GOD IS WITH YOU

God Is with You
Prayers for Men in Prison

LOIS SPEAR, O.P.

ST. ANTHONY MESSENGER PRESS
Cincinnati, Ohio

Unless otherwise indicated, Scripture citations are taken from the *New Revised Standard Version Bible*, copyright ©1989 by the Division of Christian Education of the National Council of Churches of Christ in the U.S.A. and used by permission.

Excerpts from *The New Jerusalem Bible*, copyright ©1985, are used by permission of Darton, Longman & Todd, Ltd., and Doubleday & Company, Inc.

Front cover photo copyright © Bill Fritsch/Brand X Pictures
Cover design by Mary Alfieri
Book format and design by Sandy L. Digman

ISBN 0-86716-479-4

Library of Congress Cataloging-in-Publication Data

Spear, Lois, 1920-
 God is with you: prayers for men in prison / Lois Spear.
    p. cm.
  ISBN 0-86716-479-4 (pbk.)
  1. Prisoners—Prayer-books and devotions—English. I. Title.
  BV4595 .S64 2002
  242'.68—dc21

                              2001008282

Published by St. Anthony Messenger Press
www.AmericanCatholic.org
Printed in the U.S.A.

CONTENTS

PART THREE

Peace through Acceptance and Self-Help

PART FOUR

People, Places and Events

PART FIVE

Life on the Outside

PREFACE

Although this book is meant for prisoners, their family and friends, the hope is that it will reach a wider audience. People of compassion will find, after reading these prison stories, that prisoners—no matter how heinous their crimes—are human beings just like the rest of us. God loves prisoners with the abundant love lavished on all creation. If God loves prisoners, then so must we.

In a way, we are all prisoners, trapped in our cultural backgrounds, our prejudices, addictions and fears. May this book inspire you to look beyond the prison you may have built around yourself and find that God's redemptive love extends to everyone, even those behind prison bars.

Dear Prisoner,

Bookstores today carry a large selection of books on prisons and the best way to operate them, a sign of the increasing number of prisoners and the high cost of imprisonment. Few, if any, of these books are meant for you and your spiritual and emotional well-being. This book gives you a way to look at your life and find what choices led you to where you are today. It is meant for all prisoners, from those who hope for parole in a few months or years to those who may spend the rest of their lives in prison.

You may have already looked back on your past life and the choices that brought you to prison. If not, before you begin reading this book, please spend time reflecting on your past. The look backward is not so much to blame yourself as to help you see more clearly how God has worked in your life. Yet you can't look back forever, blaming yourself or others for the bad choices you made. It is time to move ahead! You are a human being whose God delights in your creation. With God's help, you can become the person God wants you to be.

This book helps you deal with the day-to-day events of prison life. As you read the twenty-seven reflections and the Bible stories that go with them, you will see that God is with you every minute of every day.

The stories are set in a state medium-security prison in Adrian, Michigan. They are true stories as told by a prison volunteer. In addition to prisoners' stories, there are stories about the people who work in the prison or visit it. Some stories tell about life after parole. Although set in a men's prison, women prisoners should be able to see themselves in the stories. Each reflection ends with a prayer and an activity. The activities won't work in all prisons. Rules may differ from one prison to another. All of the activities, however, have been tried at one time or another by medium-security prisoners.

As you read this book, keep in mind your family and friends who suffer while you are in prison. They need you as a spouse, parent, breadwinner, sibling or friend. Your absence tears at the fabric of your life together. Pray for them. Pray also for prison staff. Ask God to help them keep their sense of human dignity by treating prisoners and everyone they meet as people worthy of respect.

Finally, pray for yourself and other prisoners, especially those who may not be guilty of any crime. By your kindness and respect, you let them know that God loves them, the people society fears and avoids. Jesus tells us (Matthew 25:31-40) that at the end of the world he will place on his right hand those who helped the misfits and the rejected: "...just as you did it to one of the least of these who are members of my family, you did it to me" (25:40).

While you are in prison, reach out to others. Jesus loves everyone. He had all of us in mind—those physically in prison and those in the prison of their own fears and hatreds—when he said: "I was in prison and you visited me...Come, you that are blessed by my Father, inherit the kingdom prepared for you from the foundation of the world" (Matthew 25:36, 34).

Go in peace to do God's work.

Sr. Lois Spear, O.P.

PART ONE

The Terrible Reality of Freedom Lost

In God alone there is rest for my soul;

from him comes my safety;

he alone is my rock, my safety,

my stronghold so that I stand unshaken.

—Psalm 62:1-2, THE NEW JERUSALEM BIBLE

Adam

We don't know his real name, so we'll call him Adam. He sits in a narrow holding pen, steel wire on two sides, glass windows on the other two. He sits alone and helpless, everything he owns in a bundle at his feet. Time changes for him only when the officers enter the holding pen to handcuff his feet and hands before taking him to a strange new place. Adam has lost his past; he's just a prison number. Life goes on around him, but he is not part of it. He feels lost and useless. He can't make any choices for himself.

SCRIPTURE READING

> ...standing near the cross of Jesus were his mother and his mother's sister, Mary the wife of Clopas, and Mary Magdalene. When Jesus saw his mother and the disciple whom he loved standing beside her, he said to his mother, "Woman, behold your son." Then he said to the disciple, "Here is your mother." And from that hour the disciple took her into his home.
>
> After this, when Jesus knew that all was now finished, he said (in order to fulfill the scripture), "I am thirsty." A jar full of sour wine was standing there. So they put a sponge full of the wine on a branch of hyssop and held it to his mouth. When Jesus had received the wine, he said, "It is finished." Then he bowed his head and gave up his spirit. (John 19:25-30)

REFLECTION

Everyone has times of feeling alone and helpless. A son or daughter gets sick and we can do nothing to help; we lose our jobs because the economy is weak. Like all of us, Adam is not totally helpless. His body may be in prison, but his spirit can go anywhere it chooses to roam. He can begin to see the wrong turns, bad choices and foolish acts that placed him on the road to prison.

The Bible tells the story of Paul, whose choices also led to prison. But Paul wanted to go there! He was following Christ. He chose to go to prison, even to die, for the love of Christ. Adam, and everyone who chooses to follow Christ, can walk the way of Paul. We can choose Christ, and with Christ as our friend, we can face life knowing that we have a place in God's love. We don't need to feel lonely or lost.

PRAYER

When you feel lonely, ask God to help you. Think of Mary, God's mother. She must have felt sad and lonely as she stood beneath the cross and watched her son die (John 19:25-30). She couldn't help him at all! Think of yourself as kneeling beside Mary at the foot of the cross. Ask Mary to help you in the way she helped Jesus when he was a child, and later, during his life of service. Look up at the face of the dying Christ. Tell him you love him and are sorry for the sins that caused this awful death. Then turn to the Good Thief hanging at Jesus' right. Ask him to pray for you. Spend time in silent prayer with Mary, Jesus and the Good Thief.

ACTIVITY

- Every time you feel lonely and lost today, pray silently the words of Jesus to the Good Thief, "Truly I tell you, today you will be with me in Paradise" (Luke 23:43).

- Look for signs around you that show God's loving care. These could be the smile of a friend, the beauty of a fallen leaf or a lovely song on the radio.

Daniel

Daniel is a small, jumpy man who often tells the officers what he thinks they are doing wrong. Daniel's mouth got him into trouble, and he was sent to another prison. Before he left Adrian, he took a history class taught by a volunteer. On the last day of class, when other students were waiting to get their certificates and perhaps a bookmark for their work, Daniel gave the volunteer a pen from the prison store. The gift was a small one. A prisoner doesn't have much money, so for Daniel, it was a big gift indeed!

When he went to another prison, Daniel began giving even bigger gifts. He started writing to pen pals in other countries. When he learned that they needed English books, he found a company that would sell them at half price. Daniel wrote to friends in this country. He asked them to buy the books and mail them to his pen pals. For his part, Daniel would pay for the books by sending his friends five dollars a month. The plan didn't work out, but it showed that Daniel is the kind of person who would spend his last cent to help his friends.

In giving gifts to others, Daniel gave gifts to himself. He no longer had time to think about himself and his problems. Through his pen pals, he learned more about the world. From the company selling books at half price, he learned that not all business people are money-grabbers.

SCRIPTURE READING

So [Elijah] set out and went to Zarephath. When he came to the gate of the town, a widow was there gathering sticks; he called to her and said, "Bring me a little water in a vessel, so that I may drink." As she was going to bring it, he called out to her and said, "Bring me a morsel of bread in your hand." But she said, "As the LORD your God lives, I have nothing baked, only a handful of meal in a jar, and a little oil in a jug; I am now gathering a couple of sticks, so that I may go home and prepare it for myself and my son, that we may eat it, and die." Elijah said to her, "Do not be afraid; go and do as you have said; but first make me a little cake of it and bring it to me, and afterwards make something for yourself and your son. For thus says the LORD the God of Israel: The jar of meal will not be emptied and the jug of oil will not fail until the day that the LORD sends rain on the earth." She went and did as Elijah said, so that she as well as he and her household ate for many days. The jar of meal was not emptied, neither did the jug of oil fail, according to the word of the LORD that he spoke by Elijah. (1 Kings 17:10-16)

REFLECTION

The Bible (1 Kings 17:8-16) tells the story of Elijah who went to a poor widow's home to ask for water and a bit of bread. He found her picking up sticks for a fire to bake the last of her flour and oil. She wanted to use the bread to feed herself and her son. Even though she and her son were very hungry, she shared her food with Elijah. God blessed the widow by keeping the jar of flour and the jug of oil full until the rains came, and the land was green again.

Unlike the widow, Daniel didn't give away his last meal. He had plenty to eat. Yet Daniel's kindness, like that of the widow's, was a small return for the great goodness of God. God has given us the free gifts of life and a beautiful world in which to grow into loving people.

When we stand before God empty-handed, our prayers should be filled with wonder and thanksgiving for these great gifts. All too often, however, we just ask for more gifts, some of them not good for us. We need to ask for God's help, of course, when we feel lonely and unloved. Yet our most heartfelt prayers must always be words of praise and thanksgiving.

PRAYER

Read this prayer of thanksgiving. After each phrase say, "I thank you, God." Then add your own prayers of thanksgiving.

For making our beautiful world, I thank you, God.
For giving me life, I thank you, God.
For blessing me with family and friends, I thank you, God.
For loving me even when I act in unloving ways,
    I thank you, God.
For forgiving me when I have sinned against you,
    I thank you, God.
For being always at my side, I thank you, God. AMEN.

ACTIVITY

- Think about how you spend the money you earn at your prison job. You could set aside a little money each week to help others, poor children, for example.

- Ask the activities director about having a relay for the food bank in town. The relay is easy. Volunteers ask for money for the food bank. In return, they walk around the yard for an hour or so. The walk may seem like a waste of time, but it's a way to use our bodies as part of the gifts we are giving. For the relay to work, you will need the help of prison staff and lots of volunteers. Begin by making posters asking for help, both from staff and prisoners. Next, meet with volunteers to plan the relay. Have sign-up sheets ready so volunteers can choose what they want to do—be relay workers, walkers or both. To avoid problems, ask the activities director to take any money you raise and give it to the food bank. After the relay, thank everyone who helped make it a success.

Blaine

Blaine is an angry man. He's friendly on the outside, but inside his heart is full of anger. He writes, "Prison has shown me that laws are used only as a way to get ahead. Jobs mean more than human rights. Only a few people are treated fairly. People think they're great when they run down everyone they meet. Lying, stealing, cheating and killing are all right when you're rich. They're wrong if you're poor."

Blaine is so angry that he can't see the many good people around him. He can't see the good in the chaplain, volunteers, staff and other prisoners.

Blaine is right, however, when he talks about injustice. Our prisons are filled with the poor, those who can't read and people of minority races. People who aren't guilty have been sent to prison and even to death row. We also find injustice in other places besides prison. Think of young children across the world who die of hunger every day. In places where war is going on, poor people die by the hundreds. Many of them die because they believe in Jesus or because of the color of their skin.

SCRIPTURE READING

> Then [Jesus] entered the temple and began to drive out those who were selling things there; and he said, "It is written,
>
> > 'My house shall be a house of prayer';
> > but you have made it a den of robbers."
>
> Every day he was teaching in the temple. The chief

priests, the scribes, and the leaders of the people kept looking for a way to kill him; but they did not find anything they could do, for all the people were spellbound by what they heard. (Luke 19:45-48)

REFLECTION

How can we help people who aren't treated fairly? The Bible (Psalm 140) says, "I know that the LORD maintains the cause of the needy, and executes justice for the poor." We have a right to get angry when we see people who aren't being treated fairly. Jesus became angry when he saw people selling goods at the temple (Luke 19:45-46). They were cheating the people! He drove them out of the temple. But Jesus didn't stay angry. If you keep thinking about something that's not fair, you'll never get over it. If you stay angry, you only hurt yourself.

PRAYER

Take a walk around the yard today. As you walk, pray the words of the Good Thief as he hung on the cross beside Jesus:

Jesus, remember me when you come into your kingdom (Luke 23:42). AMEN.

ACTIVITY

- Think of someone whom you could have hurt in some way. Write or talk to that person and say you are sorry.

- In the library read about one place in the world where people are suffering because of war. It could be Iraq, Rwanda, Kosovo or Afghanistan. After you read about this place, write to your representative in Congress. Ask if something can be done to help stop the fighting.

Jeff

Jeff was one of the first prisoners to sign up for a journalism class. He was the editor of a new prison newspaper.

Jeff quickly got into trouble. He was very proud of his new job. The other prisoners didn't like it when Jeff wouldn't take stories they had written for the newspaper. The real trouble came when Jeff began looking into the Inmates' Prison Fund. The fund was meant to help prisoners, but Jeff said it wasn't doing that. He planned to write a story so that everyone would know the truth. A few days later, Jeff was sent to a maximum-security prison. He had made too many enemies, the officers said.

At the new prison, the officers found a knife hidden in one of Jeff's bags. Someone had planted the knife there to get even with him, the officers decided.

SCRIPTURE READING

[Jesus] also told this parable to some who trusted in themselves that they were righteous and regarded others with contempt: "Two men went up to the temple to pray, one a Pharisee and the other a tax collector. The Pharisee, standing by himself, was praying thus, 'God, I thank you that I am not like other people: thieves, rogues, adulterers, or even like this tax collector. I fast twice a week; I give a tenth of all my income.' But the tax collector, standing far off, would not even look up to heaven, but was beating his breast and saying, 'God, be merciful to me, a sinner!' I tell you, this man went down to his home justified rather than the other; for all who exalt themselves will be humbled, but all who humble themselves will be exalted." (Luke 18:9-14)

REFLECTION

It's wrong to try to get even with someone you don't like. Before doing something like that, it's best to stop and think of what might be the result. Ask yourself: Is this a good act or just a way of getting even? What about Jeff and the way he acted? He could have tried to find out why people didn't like him; then he could have changed the way he acted. His pride got him in trouble; he couldn't see the truth until it was too late.

In the Bible (Luke 18:9-14), Jesus tells about two people—a Pharisee and a tax collector—who went into the temple to pray. The Pharisee couldn't hear God's voice because he was too busy talking about himself. He was proud of being a priest in the temple. He was glad he wasn't like the other man, a tax collector. "He collects taxes and everybody hates him!" the Pharisee thought. When the tax collector prayed, all he said was "God, be merciful to me, a sinner!" Jesus liked the prayer of the tax collector; he did not like the prayer of the Pharisee.

We all act like the Pharisee sometimes. Think of a time when you were glad you weren't like someone else. It could have been someone you and your friends looked down on. Did you ever lose a ballgame and then try to get even with the winners?

PRAYER

Think of yourself as the tax collector kneeling in the temple. Pray these words:

My God, I love you. Help me to see myself as I am, a sinner in need of your mercy. Forgive me for the times I have sinned in my pride. Help the people I have hurt by what I have done. Help me to be strong and not to try to get even with people who have hurt my feelings. Bless Jeff and prisoners like him. Help them to see that you love them, even when they sin. AMEN.

ACTIVITY

- Write or think about a new ending to Jeff's story. Show how he could have been a better editor by listening to other people and their ideas.

- The next time you write to your family or call them, don't use too many "I" words. Too many "I"s can make you seem proud and not willing to listen to what your family has to say.

James

When you first meet him, James seems like a quiet, peaceful man. But his eyes, seen from behind glasses with thick lenses, look a little strange. On the whole, however, he is clean and neat, polite and kind.

The teacher and prisoners in James's class see another side of him. He is touchy and half angry. When other prisoners call him "bird," the English word for his French last name, he gets upset. At other times, he likes to talk to the class. When he gets the floor, he doesn't make too much sense. He uses words he's heard in class, like "jurisdiction" or "statutory." He ends with one of these sayings: "we, the people"; "it all goes back to the Bank of England"; or "did you know that the Federal Reserve is privately owned?"

The prisoners and the teacher don't see James in the same way. The teacher is upset with James. She wants to get back to the subject she is teaching. James doesn't know what he did wrong. He just wanted to talk to the class! The other students know what's going on; they've seen people act like that before. They know that James has mental problems. He should be in a hospital, not a prison. But nobody wants him, so the prison has become his home.

SCRIPTURE READING

> On the way to Jerusalem Jesus was going through the
> region between Samaria and Galilee. As he entered a
> village, ten lepers approached him. Keeping their
> distance, they called out, saying, "Jesus, Master, have
> mercy on us!" When he saw them, he said to them, "Go
> and show yourselves to the priests." And as they went,
> they were made clean. Then one of them, when he saw
> that he was healed, turned back, praising God with a loud
> voice. He prostrated himself at Jesus' feet and thanked
> him. And he was a Samaritan. Then Jesus asked, "Were
> not ten made clean? But the other nine, where are they?
> Was none of them found to return and give praise to God
> except this foreigner?" Then he said to him, "Get up and
> go on your way; your faith has made you well."
> (Luke 17:11-19)

REFLECTION

In the Bible (Luke 17:11-19), Jesus tells the story of ten lepers
who came to see him. They stayed far away from Jesus and
called out to him. That was the law! People who had leprosy, the
AIDS of their time, looked terrible. They could be missing an ear
or part of a nose. People who didn't have leprosy were afraid of
them. They thought lepers were great sinners who should stay
far away from people who weren't sick.

Jesus wasn't afraid of lepers. He cured them and then said,
"Go and show yourselves to the priest." The lepers, except for
the one who came back to say thank you, walked with great happiness along the road back to their family and friends.

Like the lepers in the Bible story, James is someone most
people don't want to be around. "He's strange and he talks
funny," they say. Yet Jesus loves James and all the people we run

away from because they aren't like us.

PRAYER

> *Lord Jesus, I ask you to bless James and all people who have no friends because they are sick in body or mind. Help me to be kind to people who don't act like me. You love everyone you made, Jesus. Help me to love as you did.* AMEN.

ACTIVITY

- Watch for the Jameses you may meet today. Be kind to them. Listen to them, even if they don't make sense.

- In the library, try to find out how many mentally sick people are in prison. Write to your representative and ask if something can be done to help these people.

Edward

Volunteer teachers hope Edward won't take their class. Edward likes to talk, and he talks about everything. Sometimes he repeats what someone else has just said. He offends volunteers by talking about their weight and the clothes they wear. He shows off before the other prisoners. "I talked back to the officers," he brags.

Edward wants to help volunteers, but he isn't careful about keeping prison rules. One evening, for example, he put a homemade flower in a volunteer's briefcase. That breaks the rule that volunteers can take out of the prison only what they bring in.

Edward's problem is that he hasn't adjusted to prison life. Most prisoners blend in like green leaves on a tree. Edward sticks out like a bright yellow leaf. He bragged about his model ships and brought the biggest one to class. The officer took it away from him. "It's too big; it breaks prison rules," the officer said. He sent the ship home to Edward's family.

SCRIPTURE READING

> Consider your own call, brothers and sisters: not many of you were wise by human standards, not many were powerful, not many were of noble birth. But God chose what is foolish in the world to shame the wise; God chose what is weak in the world to shame the strong; God chose what is low and despised in the world, things that are not, to reduce to nothing things that are, so that no one might boast in the presence of God. He is the source of your life in Christ Jesus, who became for us wisdom from God, and righteousness and sanctification and redemption, in order that, as it is written, "Let the one who boasts, boast in the Lord." (1 Corinthians 1:26-31)

REFLECTION

In the Bible (1 Corinthians 1:26-31), we are told that God has chosen us. God didn't choose us because we can live well with other people. God chose us because we are weak and sinful. God chose us as an act of pure love. We have nothing to brag about but God's love.

Edward is one of God's chosen ones. God has a special love for people whom the world doesn't like because they are different.

PRAYER

Think of Edward and all prisoners who can't get used to life in prison. Then pray these words from the Bible (Ephesians 1:3-8):

Blessed be the God and Father of our Lord Jesus Christ, who has blessed us in Christ with every spiritual blessing in the heavenly places, just as he chose us in Christ before the foundation of the world to be holy and blameless before him in love.... In [Christ] we have redemption through his blood, the forgiveness of our trespasses, according to the riches of his grace that he lavished on us. AMEN.

ACTIVITY

- Learn this sentence from the Bible: "Let the one who boasts, boast in the Lord" (1 Corinthians 1:31). When you feel like bragging, say these words to yourself.

- Find out if the library has any books on personality types, like the Myers-Briggs Type Indicator. The indicator is a test that helps you learn more about yourself. It can also show you why other people don't act like you. Ask the librarian to help you take the test. It will help you get along better in prison.

PART TWO

A Tragic Longing
for Freedom

All you who pass this way,

look and see:

is any sorrow like the sorrow

inflicted on me,

with which Yahweh struck me

on the day of his burning anger?

—Lamentations 1:12, The New Jerusalem Bible

Vitomir

Vitomir Hinic was an average prisoner, the warden said. Yet his life ended in a ditch on Parr Highway across the street from the state prison. Vitomir's past is not clear. The newspapers didn't tell anything about his life. All people wanted to know about him was how he died. Vitomir was forty years old. He came to the United States in 1983 from what was once Yugoslavia. His parents still live there. Vitomir worked as a fisherman along the West Coast. Ten years later, he left his wife and two children in California and came to Detroit. In Detroit, the police stopped him and found that he was carrying 972 grams of cocaine. Michigan's 650 Lifer Law says that anyone carrying 650 grams or over must be given life without parole.

Vitomir spent the first year of his life sentence at the Adrian state prison. During that time, the staff called him a good prisoner. He was a small, thin man who said little and made few friends. He got little mail and had no visitors. A level-four prisoner, he should have stayed in close security. He shouldn't have held a prison job, such as working in the kitchen. Yet on December 25, 1994, Vitomir asked to help in the kitchen after Christmas dinner and was told he could do so.

Vitomir didn't plan to run away, the warden said. He didn't ask other prisoners to help him; he worked alone. When the other prisoners were cleaning up the kitchen, Vitomir slipped out a side door. He climbed two fences with razor wire on top. He ran across Parr Highway with blood on his hands, face and clothes. An officer, seeing Vitomir, called his name. He stopped, looked at the officer and kept on running. He died from bullet wounds to his back.

SCRIPTURE READING

The LORD is my shepherd, I shall not want.
He makes me lie down in green pastures;
he leads me beside still waters;
he restores my soul.
He leads me in right paths
for his name's sake.

Even though I walk through the darkest valley,
I fear no evil;
for you are with me;
your rod and your staff—
they comfort me.

You prepare a table before me
in the presence of my enemies;
you anoint my head with oil;
my cup overflows.
Surely goodness and mercy shall follow me
all the days of my life,
and I shall dwell in the house of the LORD
my whole life long. (Psalm 23)

REFLECTION

Vitomir's silence, both in life and in death, makes it hard to know what drove him to such hopelessness. He would accept anything, even death, before the living hell of his life. It may have been the loss of his family, or he could have been sad because he was not guilty of a crime. His poor English might have made things worse. His small, thin body could have left him open to sexual attack. His hopelessness may have deepened on Christmas day, a time when people join family and friends for dinner. For the lonely, Christmas is the hardest day of the year.

The Bible tells the story of Job, a good man and rich. He has a large family and lots of land and farm animals. His neighbors like him. Yet in one day, Job loses everything. He sits among the ashes and garbage and longs for death.

> …the prisoners are at ease together;
> they do not hear the voice of the taskmaster.
> The small and the great are there,
> and the slaves are free from their masters. (Job 3:18-19)

Through Job's hopelessness runs a tiny ray of hope. He thinks of the new growth after a tree has been cut down:

> For there is hope for a tree,
> if it is cut down, that it will sprout again,
> and that its shoots will not cease. (Job 14:7)

God answered Job's prayer by giving his family and lands back to him.

Unlike Job, Vitomir felt he couldn't wait on God. After one year in prison, he tried to run away. He didn't know that five years later the 650 Lifer Law would be changed to allow prisoners to apply for parole. But Vitomir lost hope!

PRAYER

> *God of mercy and forgiveness,*
> *I ask you to bless and help the prisoners who have no hope.*
> *When everything seems dark around them,*
> *show them the light of your love.*
> *Bless me that I may always see the good in my life.*
> *Fill my heart with thankfulness and hope in your love.* AMEN.

ACTIVITY

• Learn this sentence from the Bible: "Even though I walk through the darkest valley, I fear no evil; for you are with me;

your rod and your staff—they comfort me" (Psalm 23:4). Pray the sentence when you feel hopeless.

- Make a list of your gifts. Be sure to put the gift of life at the top of your list. Read the list when you don't feel good about yourself.

- Try to help others. It could be the prisoner who never gets mail, the one who never has visitors or the one who is discouraged. Talk to them. Tell them things will get better.

- When you are discouraged, talk to the chaplain or to a good friend.

Nguyen

Everyone in Nguyen's cellblock knows his story. He tells it over and over again as if he's afraid he might forget it. Yet the story is hard to forget. A young man leaves Vietnam just before the Vietcong arrive. He knows that they will kill him for helping American troops. He gets in a rusty boat that sinks near the shores of Cambodia. Nguyen and two other men swim to shore. Guerrilla soldiers see them. Nguyen hides in the bushes and watches the guerrillas kill the two other men. He runs away from the guerrillas and finally arrives in the United States. Free at last!

Things are fine for a few years. Nguyen marries and has two children. Then trouble begins. Nguyen forgets his past and tries to get rich quick. He breaks the law and goes to prison. Now he's afraid the judge will send him back to Vietnam. If he returns, the Vietcong will kill him.

Nguyen keeps repeating his story, because he fears he will be forced to leave his family and his new country.

SCRIPTURE READING

Then Jesus said to them, "You will all become deserters because of me this night; for it is written,

'I will strike the shepherd,
  and the sheep of the flock will be scattered.'

But after I am raised up, I will go ahead of you to Galilee." Peter said to him, "Though all become deserters because of you, I will never desert you." Jesus said to him, "Truly I tell you, this very night, before the cock crows, you will deny me three times."...

Now Peter was sitting outside in the courtyard. A servant-girl came to him and said, "You also were with Jesus the Galilean." But he denied it before all of them, saying, "I do not know what you are talking about." When he went out to the porch, another servant-girl saw him, and she said to the bystanders, "This man was with Jesus of Nazareth." Again he denied it with an oath, "I do not know the man." After a little while the bystanders came up and said to Peter, "Certainly you are also one of them, for your accent betrays you." Then he began to curse, and he swore an oath, "I do not know the man!" At that moment the cock crowed. Then Peter remembered what Jesus had said: "Before the cock crows, you will deny me three times." And he went out and wept bitterly. (Matthew 26:31-35, 69-75)

REFLECTION

It's easy to see why Nguyen is afraid. We have fears, too. As children, we were afraid of ghosts in the dark. As adults, we fear for our children's safety on city streets.

The Bible, in Matthew 26:31-75, tells the story of another kind of fear. Peter had said he'd always stay with Jesus. It was a different story when Jesus stood before Herod and faced death. Peter was scared, so he told a lie. He said he'd never even heard of Jesus. A rooster crowed, and Peter knew he hadn't been a friend of Jesus. His fear had kept him from standing by Jesus when he needed him. Peter felt bad. He ran out of the courtyard and, when he was far away from everyone, he began to cry.

PRAYER

Lord, I ask you to bless the people who are afraid today. Bless people like Peter who turn away when they are afraid. Help them to turn back to you. Bless people like Nguyen who face their fears by telling their stories over and over again. Help me to face my fears with courage. AMEN.

ACTIVITY

- The other side of fear is courage. Courage grows when we try to do the right thing even when we are afraid. Today, try to practice courage in little things. Be patient when people aren't nice to you. Smile even when you have to wait in long lines to go to the library or other places where you want to go.

- Think of someone in your life who acted with courage even when afraid. Write a note of thanks to that person.

David

David is a short man who is always on the move. You'll know him when you meet him; he wears short pants and an undershirt, even in winter. He's always hot! He usually works two or more prison jobs to get a little extra money.

David doesn't like it when he sees someone not being

treated right. He does what he can to make things better. When he can't seem to help, he works off steam by jogging around the yard until he has run two miles. When he comes back, he takes a shower and then he feels better.

David has found ways to work off his anger when things don't go right for him. He draws pictures that tell funny stories about what went on. Once, when he had trouble with another prisoner, David wrote a story for his grandkids. It was all about a muskrat named Melanie and her standoff with a nasty snapping turtle named Ed. Ed, of course, was the name of the prisoner who made David angry. "After that I felt much better," David said.

David has served ten years of a thirty-year sentence as an habitual offender. He would be up for parole in another ten years, but he got more prison time for breaking rules. Breaking small rules—talking back to an officer, not having call-out slips signed, keeping the wrong things in your locker—can add to a prison term.

David might have gone on quietly serving his time, but he got bad news from the prison doctor. David had hepatitis C, the doctor said. People with the disease usually live no longer than ten years. The news upset David; he became even more active than before. He wanted to be paroled right away; he needed time with his family before he died. "I don't want to go home when all I'll be doing is giving my family someone to feed baby food to and change diapers for," he said.

David went the limit. He wrote to the judge and the parole board. He asked friends to write to the governor and state legislators. Nothing worked.

Then David made a bold move. He wrote to friends, asking them to set up a Web site for him. He planned to fill the Web site with stories about the unfair things that went on in prison. His friends would put the stories on the Web site. No one could make David see that he would get caught and have more prison time to serve. So far he hasn't been able to find anyone foolish enough to help him.

SCRIPTURE READING

Immediately [Jesus] made the disciples get into the boat and go on ahead to the other side, while he dismissed the crowds. And after he had dismissed the crowds, he went up the mountain by himself to pray. When evening came, he was there alone, but by this time the boat, battered by the waves, was far from the land, for the wind was against them. And early in the morning he came walking toward them on the sea. But when the disciples saw him walking on the sea, they were terrified, saying, "It is a ghost!" And they cried out in fear. But immediately Jesus spoke to them and said, "Take heart, it is I; do not be afraid."

Peter answered him, "Lord, if it is you, command me to come to you on the water." He said, "Come." So Peter got out of the boat, started walking on the water, and came toward Jesus. But when he noticed the strong wind, he became frightened, and beginning to sink, he cried out, "Lord, save me!" Jesus immediately reached out his hand and caught him, saying to him, "You of little faith, why did you doubt?" When they got into the boat, the wind ceased. And those in the boat worshiped him, saying, "Truly you are the Son of God." (Matthew 14:22-33)

REFLECTION

David's story is like that of Peter, one of Jesus' friends. Peter and his friends were out fishing (Matthew 14:22-33). They looked up and saw Jesus walking toward them across the water! The fishermen were afraid, but Jesus said to them: "Take heart, it is I; do not be afraid!" (Matthew 14:27). Peter wanted to do the same thing. Jesus called to him, saying, "Come." Peter got out of the boat and began walking on the water. It felt great! But then he looked down and saw all that water! He was afraid! As he began to sink, he called out, "Lord, save me!" Jesus held Peter's hand and saved him. "You of little faith," Jesus said to Peter.

David, like Peter, is a man who wants to be up and doing things. He hasn't time to wait for God. Yet God will answer our prayers and make things right if we ask God in faith. We need God's help in every problem we face, no matter how big or how little. A good way to ask for God's help is through the prayer that Jesus taught us, the Lord's Prayer.

PRAYER

Our Father who art in heaven, hallowed be thy name, thy kingdom come, thy will be done, on earth as it is in heaven. Give us this day our daily bread and forgive us our trespasses as we forgive those who trespass against us. And lead us not into temptation, but deliver us from evil. AMEN.

ACTIVITY

- When you are about to act without thinking, say this prayer: "Jesus, be with me in all I do." Then find a quiet place to sit and decide on the best thing to do.

- When something upsets you and you feel angry, try jogging around the yard or shooting a few baskets. If you can't leave your cell, do some exercises.

- To keep your spirits high, write a story or poem, start a hobby, or work in the greenhouse or flowerbed.

José

José isn't afraid to show his feelings. It's part of his Spanish culture. His first weeks in prison were very hard. He didn't know that he should have his call-out slip signed. "The guard yelled at me," he wrote, "and treated me awful in front of everyone. All I did was stand there. When I went back to my cell I cried."

José felt bad because he didn't think he belonged in prison. "I'm not guilty," he said. His counselors thought he was in denial. "I get so upset that they can't accept the fact that I am innocent," he said. "I have lost everything that I worked so hard for."

José's life fell apart when his wife divorced him and took their children. She accused José of child sexual abuse. He said he wasn't guilty, but the jury didn't believe him.

SCRIPTURE READING

They came to Jericho. As [Jesus] and his disciples and a large crowd were leaving Jericho, Bartimaeus son of Timaeus, a blind beggar, was sitting by the roadside. When he heard that it was Jesus of Nazareth, he began to shout out and say, "Jesus, Son of David, have mercy on me!" Many sternly ordered him to be quiet, but he cried out even more loudly, "Son of David, have mercy on me!" Jesus stood still and said, "Call him here." And they called the blind man, saying to him, "Take heart; get up, he is calling you." So throwing off his cloak, he sprang up and came to Jesus. Then Jesus said to him, "What do you want me to do for you?" The blind man said to him, "My teacher, let me see again." Jesus said to him, "Go; your faith has made you well." Immediately he regained his sight and followed him on the way. (Mark 10:46-52)

REFLECTION

Feelings can be very good when we control them. One of our strongest feelings is sexual love. In the Song of Solomon, the bridegroom calls:

> How beautiful you are, my love,
>   how very beautiful!
> Your eyes are doves
>   behind your veil.
> Your hair is like a flock of goats,
>   moving down the slopes of Gilead….
> Your lips are like a crimson thread,
>   and your mouth is lovely.
> You are altogether beautiful, my love;
>   and there is no flaw in you. (4:1-7)

Feelings can have a down side, too. When they are out of control, we can hurt ourselves and those we love. Love can turn into hate; anger can become bitterness; fear can become cowardice. We need to be very careful of our feelings when in prison. Anyone who shows strong feelings can be seen as weak.

The Bible tells the story of the blind man Bartimaeus (Mark 10:46-52). When Jesus walked by him, Bartimaeus called out, "Son of David, have mercy on me!" He didn't stop calling until Jesus came to him and asked, "What do you want me to do for you?" "My teacher, let me see again," the blind man called. Jesus restored his sight.

Jesus can help us, too. He can teach us to use our feelings in ways that are good. We just have to ask him.

PRAYER

Tell Jesus that you need his help. Read the prayer needs below. After each one, say the words of Bartimaeus: "Son of David, have pity on me!"

> Lord, that I may see! Son of David, have pity on me!
>
> Lord, when I feel angry, help me to see the good in whatever I'm angry about. Son of David, have pity on me!
>
> Lord, when I feel sad, help me to think of times when I was happy. Son of David, have pity on me!
>
> Lord, when I feel afraid, help me to face my fears honestly. Son of David, have pity on me!
>
> Lord, when I want to love and hold someone, help me to be grateful for the people who love me. Son of David, have pity on me!
>
> Lord, help me to use my feelings to help others. Son of David, have pity on me. AMEN.

ACTIVITY

- Pretend you are Bartimaeus. Call out silently to Jesus as he walks by your prison cell. What will you ask Jesus to give you? Freedom? Money? Drugs? A sexual partner? Why not ask for more faith? More patience? More understanding?

- Find a notebook that you can use for writing down your thoughts. Write down ways to help control your feelings. Here are some ideas. If you are angry, pray for the person who angered you. If you want sex, do some exercises or ask to work in the yard. If you are afraid, find someone you can trust.

- Some people around you may be bullied or used for sex. Help them if you can.

Patrick

Patrick is hard to forget. He's a tall, well-built man with a huge Afro and an angry look on his face. But that's just the way he looks on the outside. When Patrick meets people he likes and trusts, he gives them a warm smile and a high five. He is a good man who loves to talk about his family in Mississippi. He dreams of the dinner his mother will fix when he comes home from prison. There will be chitterlings, fried chicken, okra and black-eyed peas.

Patrick wears an angry mask to keep him safe from sexual attack or thieves who might steal the few things he owns. The mask also hides Patrick's weakness. He can barely read and can't write more than his own name. Because he can't read, he doesn't know about new rules posted on the bulletin board. He gets detention for breaking the new rules. He is now on top security and will soon be sent to a maximum-security prison. Patrick doesn't know what he has done wrong. He only knows that it will be a long time before he will see his family in Mississippi.

SCRIPTURE READING

[Jesus] began to speak first to his disciples, "Beware of the yeast of the Pharisees, that is, their hypocrisy. Nothing is covered up that will not be uncovered, and nothing secret that will not become known. Therefore whatever you have said in the dark will be heard in the light, and what you have whispered behind closed doors will be proclaimed from the housetops.

"I tell you, my friends, do not fear those who kill the body, and after that can do nothing more. But I will warn you whom to fear: fear him who, after he has killed, has authority to cast into hell. Yes, I tell you, fear him! Are not five sparrows sold for two pennies? Yet not one of them is forgotten in God's sight. But even the hairs of your head are all counted. Do not be afraid; you are of more value than many sparrows.

"And I tell you, everyone who acknowledges me before others, the Son of Man also will acknowledge before the angels of God; but whoever denies me before others will be denied before the angels of God...."
(Luke 12:1-9)

REFLECTION

Everyone wears a mask at times. The mask hides our weaknesses. Think of the man who cries at a sad movie. He hides his tears by saying that he has something in his eyes! Masks aren't always worn for good reasons. They can be used to hurt people. Think of the person who appears to be a friend, yet tells jokes that poke sly fun at another person's differences, the way he walks or talks.

The Bible tells a story about the Pharisees (Luke 11:37-54). They hid their real reason for asking questions behind the mask of being holy men. Jesus didn't wear a mask: he spoke honestly to the Pharisees. When they asked him about his teachings, Jesus knew they didn't want to learn anything. They just wanted to catch him and then put him to death. Jesus could see what the masks hid.

As Jesus walked the lonely Way of the Cross, no one came to help him, except Simon of Cyrene (see Mark 15:21-21). Simon didn't want to be there; he'd rather have been miles away! As he walked the few steps behind Jesus, did Simon's mask ever slip, showing what lay behind it—fear, shame, anger? Or did Simon find that helping Jesus had become a labor of love? We'll never know the truth about Simon, but it may help us to think about our own lives—the masks we wear and the good people who've helped us carry our cross.

PRAYER

Share with Jesus the masks you wear and why. Ask him to help you:

— *Make your mask show the goodness within you.*
— *Carry your cross just as Simon helped Jesus carry his.*
— *Thank the people in your life who've helped you carry the cross of imprisonment.*
— *Feel sorrow for the people you have hurt.*
— *Forgive the people who have hurt you.*

ACTIVITY

• Ask your prison activities director to help you with this four-step activity.

• Write a play about a fight between Good and Evil. Have it take place in prison. Be sure the good guys win!

• Make masks for the actors—Good, Evil, a man who is in trouble and a storyteller. The masks can be made of eight-by-ten-inch sheets of stiff paper with holes cut out for the eyes and mouth. Tape the masks to a pencil, so they can be held in front of the face. You may want to make paper maché masks. They aren't hard. You'll need a bag of cut-up newspapers, flour and a large pan for mixing them together. Mix flour and water into a stiff paste. Soak the paper in the mix and squeeze out extra water. Press the wet paper into the shapes of four faces and let them dry. When they are dry, paint them with watercolors and paste decorations on them, such as feathers or leaves. After you finish, be sure to clean up the mess you've made!

- Ask if you and your friends can give the play for prisoners in your cellblock.

- Ask if the masks can be put in the prison showcase or in the library after you've given the play.

Cellblock 5

It was very hot on that August evening in 1996. Then the thunder rolled and lightning flashed. Lights went out all over the city. In a short while, sirens sounded. Everyone in Adrian knew that meant trouble at the prison. No one found out what was going on until hours later. A riot had broken out. It didn't end until early the next day.

The riot began after the lights went out. Prisoners in the yard were told to go back to their cells. The prisoners in Cellblock 5 refused to move. The cells were too hot and stuffy, they said. Prison rules said that six inches of open window and three inches above the doorframe were enough air for a prison cell. When the officers told the prisoners to move inside, they began throwing whatever was handy. They tore out toilets, broke windows and pulled out wires. Two more cellblocks joined in. It took the officers—with the help of city police and state troopers—ten hours to stop the rioting.

The riot had terrible results. Some police officers were hurt, one by a prisoner who threw his microwave at him. Damage to the prison came to at least $100,000. Damage to prisoners in the cellblock was harder to count, but it was far more serious. Some prisoners were hurt and needed a doctor. Riot leaders were sent to maximum-security prisons. Those who stayed behind faced charges of starting a riot. The charges could lead to loss of credits toward early release, the right to walk in the yard, to visit the library or gym. Whatever money the rioters had could be taken away from them. For everyone who took part, the riot was a very foolish action that helped no one.

SCRIPTURE READING

When Jesus saw the crowds, he went up the mountain; and after he sat down, his disciples came to him. Then he began to speak, and taught them, saying:

> "Blessed are the poor in spirit, for theirs is the kingdom of heaven.
>
> "Blessed are they who mourn, for they will be comforted.
>
> "Blessed are the meek, for they will inherit the earth.
>
> "Blessed are those who hunger and thirst for righteousness, for they will be filled.
>
> "Blessed are the merciful, for they will receive mercy.
>
> "Blessed are the pure in heart, for they will see God.
>
> "Blessed are the peacemakers, for they will be called children of God.
>
> "Blessed are they who are persecuted for righteousness' sake, for theirs is the kingdom of heaven.
>
> "Blessed are you when people revile you and persecute you and utter all kinds of evil against you falsely on my account. Rejoice and be glad, for your reward is great in heaven, for in the same way they persecuted the prophets who were before you...." (Matthew 5:1-11)

REFLECTION

It's hard to stand on the sidelines when a mob has taken over. It's easy to make a bad choice and join the mob. "I can't be blamed; I'm just part of a gang," we tell ourselves. "No one will catch me." But God sees us, no matter how hard we try to hide.

In the Bible (Matthew 5:1-11), Jesus tells about the happy

ones who have chosen to live in justice and peace. They are blessed by God. Read these beatitudes (blessings) below that are paraphrases of Jesus' beatitudes in Matthew 5, and think of people you know who are blessed by God because of the lives they lead.

> Happy those who hunger and thirst for what is right: they shall have their fill.
> Happy the merciful: they shall have mercy shown them.
> Happy the peacemakers: they shall be called children of God.
> Happy those who suffer in the cause of right: theirs is the kingdom of heaven.

PRAYER

God wants us to make wise choices. Ask for wisdom as you pray these words from Wisdom of Solomon 9:1-10:

> . . . Lord of mercy,
> who have made all things by your word,
> and by your wisdom have formed humankind
> to have dominion over the creatures you have made,
> and rule the world in holiness and righteousness...
> give me the wisdom that sits by your throne,
> and do not reject me from among your servants....
> With you is wisdom, she who knows your works
> and was present when you made the world;
> she understands what is pleasing in your sight....
> Send her forth from the holy heavens...
> that I may learn what is pleasing to you. AMEN.

ACTIVITY

- Keep a record of the people you've talked to today and what you said. When you have time, think about what you wrote.

Could your words have made someone angry with others? Or could your words have helped someone to make a wise choice?

- Try making a drawing of the four beatitudes in this reflection. Write a short story about each one and what it means to you. Show the drawings to your chaplain, family and friends.

- In the library, find pictures showing people living the Beatitudes. Then find a picture showing what happens when people get mixed up in riots. The newspapers are full of this kind of story! Make copies of the pictures. Paste them in your notebook, and look at them when you need to make a wise choice.

PART THREE

Peace through Acceptance and Self-Help

Bring back, Yahweh, our people from captivity

like torrents in the Negeb!

Those who sow in tears

sing as they reap.

—Psalm 126:4-5, THE NEW JERUSALEM BIBLE

LaSalle

"Hujambo, dada! Qwaheri, bwana!" Prisoners sometimes yell these words across the prison yard. They're simple Swahili words like, "Hello, sister," or "Goodbye, brother." There is a human story behind them.

LaSalle is in the thirty-ninth year of a life sentence. He hopes to be free someday. In his first years in prison, he decided that he needed God. He became a Muslim and began studying the Koran. LaSalle decided to use what he had learned as a way to help others. He didn't want to be busy just to forget his troubles. He wanted to make life better for other prisoners.

He began by preparing himself through prayer. He studied Swahili, the language spoken by many Africans. He had always wanted to learn the language. Today, LaSalle teaches two classes in Swahili. His classes have helped hundreds of prisoners find their African roots. LaSalle prays that some day he will be able to visit Africa. He wants to speak to people in the language he loves.

SCRIPTURE READING

When [Jesus] returned to Capernaum after some days, it was reported that he was at home. So many gathered around that there was no longer room for them, not even in front of the door; and he was speaking the word to them. Then some people came, bringing to him a paralyzed man, carried by four of them. And when they could not bring him to Jesus because of the crowd, they removed the roof above him; and after having dug through it, they let down the mat on which the paralytic lay. When Jesus saw their faith, he said to the paralytic, "Son, your sins are forgiven." Now some of the scribes were sitting there, questioning in their hearts, "Why does this fellow speak in this way? It is blasphemy! Who can forgive sins but God alone?" At once Jesus perceived in his spirit that they were discussing these questions among themselves; and he said to them, "Why do you raise such questions in your hearts? Which is easier, to say to the paralytic, 'Your sins are forgiven,' or to say, 'Stand up and take your mat and walk?' But so that you may know that the Son of Man has authority on earth to forgive sins"— he said to the paralytic—"I say to you, stand up, take your mat, and go to your home." And he stood up, and immediately took the mat and went out before all of them; so that they were amazed and glorified God, saying, "We have never seen anything like this!" (Mark 2:1-12)

REFLECTION

Have you ever noticed that the busiest and happiest people always have time to help others? They know that people are God's greatest gift. By helping others, these busy people tell the story of God's love for us. Their lives make us think of the paralyzed man in the Bible (Mark 2:1-12). His friends took him to Jesus, but they couldn't get him in the house. The crowd was too large! So they cut a hole in the roof. They put the paralytic on a stretcher and let him down through the roof.

PRAYER

Place yourself in God's presence. Think about the paralyzed man. How happy he must have been to have good friends! Turn and look at Jesus. He must have been surprised to see the paralytic. Think about the men carrying the stretcher. How kind they were! Next, think about LaSalle and how he has helped so many people. Ask Jesus to help you be a good friend to others as you pray:

> *Dear Jesus, help me to see the needs of people around me. Be*
> *with me as I try to help those who need me. Bless people like*
> *LaSalle and the stretcher carriers. They make life better for all of*
> *us.* AMEN.

ACTIVITY

- Think of what you could do to help other prisoners. Could you teach a class or coach a baseball team? Could you write a letter for someone or read aloud a chapter of a novel?

- Put your name on the library call-out sheet. At the library, find a book or article on Nelson Mandela, the South African freedom fighter. He spent thirty years in prison for his beliefs. Find out how he used his time in prison.

Tim

Tim is a person who knows how to use his prison time. He reads everything he can get his hands on. While in prison, he learned how to tell stories. In a class on storytelling, he told the story of Ali Baba and the Forty Thieves. You could have heard a pin drop in the class!

Tim could have spent his time in prison thinking only about the bad things in his life. He could have kept away from other prisoners. Instead, with the help of a Buddhist monk who visited him, he began setting aside time each day to reflect on the gift of loving-kindness. To get rid of anger and bitterness, Tim wrote, "I think the main thing is to think of something good and peaceful. It's slow, daily work—thinking about love and happiness and how good they make you feel."

Good thoughts aren't something from another world, Tim wrote. They're down-to-earth. It helps to have a bigger picture. "It can be a Christ picture, maybe a Buddha picture. It helps to have a really clear picture of what you want out of life."

Another way to think of the bigger picture is by using the word "faith." Faith is like the farmer who plants a field of grain and then takes care of it. He knows the grain will grow; it will feed many people. Faith, Tim said, is a good, earthy feeling. "It leads people to walk through life with their eyes wide open."

SCRIPTURE READING

[Jesus] put before them another parable: "The kingdom of heaven is like a mustard seed that someone took and sowed in his field; it is the smallest of all the seeds, but when it has grown it is the greatest of shrubs and becomes a tree, so that the birds of the air come and make nests in its branches." (Matthew 13:31-32)

REFLECTION

In the Bible (Matthew 13:31-32), Jesus speaks of faith as a mustard seed so small you can hardly see it. Yet when fully grown it's as tall as a tree. Birds even nest in its branches!

Tim sees clearly what faith is. The Farmer God plants faith in the soil of our hearts. We must care for this gift by keeping our hearts closed to evil and darkness and open to goodness and light. It will take a lot of work to make our faith grow. The results are worth it: peace of mind, a sense of self-worth and a willingness to help others grow in faith.

PRAYER

> *Farmer God, I ask you to plant deep within the soil of my being
> the tiny seed of faith. Help me to prepare the soil with good
> and peaceful thoughts and to water it with prayer.*
>
> *Farmer God, I ask you to make my faith grow so that one day,
> like the mustard seed, it will grow into a tree that no wind
> will blow over.*
>
> *Farmer God, help me make prison a place to grow in faith. Help
> prisoners whose faith is weak.*
>
> *Farmer God, stay with me when I leave prison. Walk beside me
> into a new life as a free child of God.* AMEN.

ACTIVITY

- In your notebook draw a picture of the mustard tree with a
  bird sitting in its branches. Give names to the tree and the little bird. Every time you look at the picture, say to yourself:
  "God, help me grow in faith!"

- Plan a daily prayer schedule for yourself or simply a time of
  quiet reading. Calm yourself by thinking of something good
  that happened to you recently. When angry thoughts come to
  you, think of something else. Your quiet time will leave you
  rested and at peace.

- In the library, read more about Buddhism. Find out what parts
  of Buddhist beliefs are the same as Christian beliefs.

Audie

Audie is someone you can't miss. He can see over the heads of
the other prisoners. Even if you don't notice how tall he is—six
feet, five inches—you'll notice his big smile and his chipped

front tooth. He's a happy man who makes others feel happy. As a black man, he has made friends with John, a fearful, middle-aged white man. John is a first-timer who's afraid to talk back when other prisoners pick on him. John is happy to have Audie for a friend. "My life is peaceful," he says. "Audie is kind to me."

Many prisoners keep replaying the story of why they are in prison. They are looking for someone else to blame. But not Audie. He doesn't speak often about his past. When he does, he is direct and to the point. "I did something very wrong, and now I'm paying the price," he says.

SCRIPTURE READING

Then Jesus said to the Jews who had believed in him, "If you continue in my word, you are truly my disciples; and you will know the truth, and the truth will make you free." They answered him, "We are descendants of Abraham and have never been slaves to anyone. What do you mean by saying, 'You will be made free'?" Jesus answered them, "Very truly, I tell you, everyone who commits sin is a slave to sin. The slave does not have a permanent place in the household; the son has a place there forever. So if the Son makes you free, you will be free indeed. I know that you are descendants of Abraham; yet you look for an opportunity to kill me, because there is no place in you for my word." (John 8:31-37)

REFLECTION

Audie is at peace because he sees himself, not only through his own eyes, but also through the eyes of others. He has been wrong in the past, and he is sorry for his actions. He is ready to start again and face the future with honesty and hope. A key part of Audie's outlook is his willingness to face the truth, to rise above feelings of self-pity and the need to blame others for what he has done.

We all have blind spots in our life. We want to look on everything we have done as good. If wrong must be admitted, we often think someone else is to blame. The truth can be so blinding that we put on the dark glasses of pride to keep from seeing it.

PRAYER

Today, visit the chapel for a quiet time of prayer. If the chapel is closed, find a quiet place and sink deep into the chapel of your heart. Begin by asking God to help you know yourself. Think about what keeps you from being your true self. Is it shame because of your prison clothes? Is it fear that if your "tough guy" attitude is dropped you'll be seen as weak? Are you afraid that you won't like the person you really are?

Ask God to help you drop the fear and shame that keep you from knowing the truth about yourself. Pray these words from the Bible (John 8:31-32):

> *If you continue in my word, you are truly my disciples; and you will know the truth, and the truth will make you free.*

End your quiet time by thanking God for helping you and by asking for the grace to see yourself as you really are: a child of God loved always in spite of your faults and sins.

ACTIVITY

• Look for people around you who are happy and peaceful like Audie. Reflect on how their lives show that they are at peace with themselves.

- Try reaching out to someone of another race. It could be a simple act like helping with silverware in the cafeteria, catching a sheet of paper that slid out of another prisoner's hands, or saying "I'm sorry" after bumping into someone.

Michael

Michael is a cheerful person. He lives his faith by carefully doing the work he's asked to do. The prison staff, knowing that Michael can be trusted, has given him bigger jobs. He has helped the librarian and the chaplain. Now he works in the school office. He keeps track of students who take the GED. Passing the GED means a student has a high school equivalency degree. Michael is continuing his education by taking college classes by mail. Next year he will take four college classes.

At age thirty-three, Michael feels young, except for times when he's sad and lonely. He writes, "I must confess that while I am growing older, I still feel very young and alive. I feel as if I am as young as I was when I first came to prison, like my life had been put on hold until I could be released. There are some days when I feel regret and sorrow, which makes me feel older, but for the most part, I still feel alive. Perhaps I am moving toward maturity, but I still hope to keep the inner child."

Michael's road to prison began when he was in his twenties. He was caught with over 650 grams of cocaine. In Michigan, that means prison for life with no parole. The sentence has since been lowered to twenty-five years with possible parole. Some of the state's 125 prisoners convicted under the old law have had their prison terms reduced. They are out on parole.

Michael wrote to the parole board and asked them to look at his case again. They said no. Michael can't ask again for several years. Yet, he hasn't given up hope. He wrote to the judge and lawyers who handled the case. He asked friends to write to the parole board. Nothing succeeded.

The next few years will be hard for Michael. Yet, he's still happy and peaceful. His faith is strong. He writes, "My faith has helped me deal with these frustrations. I know that everything that happens is part of a larger plan. God wants me to be here to help others and learn what drugs have done to other people's lives. I believe that when God feels my work is done here, I will be released."

Like the mustard seed in the Bible story (Matthew 13:31-32), Michael's faith has grown during his years in prison, until now it waves high above prison walls.

SCRIPTURE READING

There was a woman who had been suffering from hemorrhages for twelve years. She had endured much under many physicians, and had spent all that she had; and she was no better, but rather grew worse. She had heard about Jesus, and came up behind him in the crowd and touched his cloak, for she said, "If I but touch his clothes, I will be made well." Immediately her hemorrhage stopped; and she felt in her body that she was healed of her disease. Immediately aware that power had gone forth from him, Jesus turned about in the crowd and said, "Who touched my clothes?" And his disciples said to him, "You see the crowd pressing in on you; how can you say, 'Who touched me?'" He looked all around to see who had done it. But the woman, knowing what had happened to her, came in fear and trembling, fell down before him, and told him the whole truth. He said to her, "Daughter, your faith has made you well; go in peace and be healed of your disease." (Mark 5:25-34)

REFLECTION

Have you ever noticed in the Bible how often Jesus, after curing someone, said, "Your faith has cured you"? Take the above story of the sick woman in Mark. She wanted to touch the hem of Jesus' clothes. Jesus cured her, saying, "Daughter, your faith has made you well."

Jesus will do the same for each of us if we have faith. He answered Michael's prayers by showing him why he is in prison and how to use his time helping others. When he leaves prison—in 2004, 2010 or 2015, who knows?—Michael will be a man of deep faith.

PRAYER

Find a place where you can sit quietly. Think about your own faith. How does your faith help you get through each day? Read this litany of faith. After each phrase say the prayer of the father of the boy with an unclean spirit in the Bible, "I believe; help my unbelief!" (Mark 9:24).

> I believe, God, that you made the world and everything in it. I believe, oh God, help my unbelief!
>
> I believe that you love me, God, as part of your beautiful world. I believe, oh God, help my unbelief!
>
> I believe, God, that you want me to be happy in this world and the next. I believe, oh God, help my unbelief!
>
> I believe that you are with me always and will help me if I ask for your help. I believe, oh God, help my unbelief!
>
> I believe, God, that you are pleased and happy when I help people in your name. I believe, oh God, help my unbelief!
>
> God, I believe in you and I love you. Help me to love you more every day. I believe, oh God, help my unbelief! AMEN.

ACTIVITY

- Take a faith walk around the yard today. When you pass other people or see beauty around you, silently thank God for the gift of sight and the beauty of nature.

- In the legal library, try to learn more about the laws you broke. Can you find court records of cases like yours? If so, show them to your lawyer.

Kinte

Kinte is a short man with big arms and shoulders. To make up for being short, he tries to be the best at everything. In a world cultures class, he wants to get the best grades on weekly tests, so he dares the class to beat him. The one with the best grades will stand tall, and the rest of the class will bow before him. When Kinte wins the dare, he smiles happily while the other prisoners bow to him.

Kinte is fun to have in class. He tells great stories! The other prisoners like him. When he went to prison, Kinte made a choice: He would always choose the good, rather than the bad. For the most part, he's kept his choice, but when he fails, he isn't a very good person. He can be mean to prisoners he doesn't like. If anyone even looks at anything he owns, Kinte gives the man an angry glare. Kinte's bad side never lasts long. He's soon cheerful again, helping other prisoners, telling jokes to the officers and asking them to walk the volunteer teacher across the yard after class.

SCRIPTURE READING

> See, I have set before you today life and prosperity, death
> and adversity. If you obey the commandments of the
> LORD your God that I am commanding you today, by
> loving the LORD your God, walking in his ways, and
> observing his commandments, decrees, and ordinances,
> then you shall live and become numerous, and the LORD,
> your God, will bless you in the land you are entering to
> possess. But if your heart turns away and you do not hear,
> but are led astray to bow down to other gods and serve
> them, I declare to you today that you shall perish; you
> shall not live long in the land that you are crossing the
> Jordan to enter and possess. I call heaven and earth to
> witness against you today that I have set before you life
> and death, blessings and curses. Choose life so that you
> and your descendants may live, loving the LORD, your
> God, obeying him, and holding fast to him; for that means
> life to you and length of days, so that you may live in the
> land that the LORD swore to give to your ancestors, to
> Abraham, to Isaac, and to Jacob. (Deuteronomy 30:15-20)

REFLECTION

Like many of us, Kinte spent years without making a choice
about his life. He didn't know that not choosing was itself a
choice: He was doing whatever was easiest. He wasn't thinking
about where his life was going.

Then one day he came to a crossroad. It may have been
when he started reading about his African ancestors. His mind
cleared; he chose to live a good life. He dropped his old name of
Donald, taking on a new name and a new life. In the years after
that, Kinte lived his choice in many ways. Sometimes, on dark
days when everything seemed to go wrong, he failed to choose

the good. Those days went by quickly and Kinte returned to his first choice.

Every day of our lives we are asked to make choices, some of them as easy as what book to read, others as hard as choosing to be fair to someone we don't like. Like Kinte, we are called to choose the good. If we ask for help, God will give us the strength to make good choices.

In the Bible (Deuteronomy 30:15-20), God tells the people: "I have set before you today life and prosperity, death and adversity.... Choose life, so that you and your descendants may live, loving the LORD your God...." As Kinte has found out, the choice must be made every hour of every day. The way of evil is wide and smooth. It's easy to let anger and other bad feelings rule our thoughts and actions. Life in prison can be very hard. It's easy to give in to hopelessness, instead of forcing the mind and will to find the good in even the worst events of the day.

PRAYER

Place yourself in God's presence. Think about the choices you made today. Did you choose life or death? Think of the choices you will make for the rest of the day. How can you make sure that they are life choices?

Read this litany of choice. After each line, pray the words: "God, help me choose life!"

When I feel down today...God, help me choose life!
When someone makes me angry...God, help me choose life!
When I'm treated as a nobody, a prison number...God, help me choose life!
When I long to be by myself...God, help me choose life!
When no one writes or visits me...God, help me choose life!
When I miss home and family...God, help me choose life!
When I have no one to talk to...God, help me choose life!

When I hate myself and everyone near me...God, help me choose life!
When I am lonely...God, help me choose life! AMEN.

ACTIVITY

- Write in your notebook the good choices you made today. Try to write in your notebook every day. When you feel down, reread what you have written.

- Look for ways to get more schooling: Visit the library; sign up for a class; ask to tutor a prisoner for the GED.

- Ask the chaplain about prayer or Bible study groups. If there are none, ask if you can start one.

PART FOUR

People, Places and Events

As the chosen of God, then, the holy people whom he loves,

you are to be clothed in heartfelt compassion,

in generosity and humility, gentleness and patience.

—Colossians 3:12, THE NEW JERUSALEM BIBLE

Michelle

Michelle walks a fine line between the needs of prisoners and prison rules. As activities director, she is in charge of volunteers and clubs, like Alcoholics Anonymous, veterans and Spanish clubs. Each day she goes through dozens of kites (notes) sent by prisoners asking for help with one activity or another. Michelle is a person who fits her job well. She is strict without being bossy; she listens to prisoners instead of saying, "We can't do that! It's against the rules." Michelle's boss likes her; her boss has found that, while being helpful with prisoners, Michelle is also careful to do her job well.

During Black History Month a few years ago, a group of prisoners asked Michelle if they could give a play they had written. Michelle knew that if she said yes it would mean a lot of work. She would have to check with her boss, find a place to give the play and make time for the players to practice together.

Michelle could have said no; it would have been a lot easier! On the other hand, she knew the play was about good values; it broke no rules. After talking to her boss, Michelle told the prisoners to begin working on the play. The chaplain let the play be given in the chapel where the setting was quiet and it was easy to hear. However, there were no curtains. Two prisoners said they'd hold up a bed sheet between acts. That would take the place of a curtain. Other prisoners made props—a paper cigar and a yardstick for a cane.

The play was a great success. Everyone in the chapel clapped for the players. They even got a standing ovation! Michelle stayed in the background. She wanted the prisoners to get all the praise.

SCRIPTURE READING

"For it is as if a man, going on a journey, summoned his slaves and entrusted his property to them; to one he gave five talents, to another two, to another one, to each according to his ability. Then he went away. The one who had received the five talents went off at once and traded with them, and made five more talents. In the same way, the one who had the two talents made two more talents. But the one who had received the one talent went off and dug a hole in the ground and hid his master's money. After a long time the master of those slaves came and settled accounts with them. Then the one who had received the five talents came forward, bringing five more talents, saying, 'Master, you handed over to me five talents; see, I have made five more talents.' His master said to him, 'Well done, good and trustworthy slave; you have been trustworthy in a few things, I will put you in charge of many things; enter into the joy of your master.' And the one with the two talents also came forward, saying, 'Master, you handed over to me two talents; see, I have made two more talents.' His master said to him, 'Well done, good and trustworthy slave; you have been trustworthy in a few things, I will put you in charge of many things; enter into the joy of your master.' Then the one who had received the one talent also came forward, saying, 'Master, I knew that you were a harsh man, reaping where you did not sow, and gathering where you did not scatter seed; so I was afraid, and I went and hid your talent in the ground. Here you have what is yours.' But his master replied, 'You wicked and lazy slave! You knew, did you, that I reap where I did not sow and gather where I did not scatter? Then you ought to have invested my money with the bankers, and on my return I would have received what was my own with interest. So take the talent from him, and give it to the one with the ten talents. For to all those who have, more will be given, and they will have an abundance; but from those who have nothing, even what they have will be taken away. As for this worthless slave, throw him into the outer darkness, where there will be weeping and gnashing of teeth.'" (Matthew 25:14-30)

REFLECTION

Everyone has God-given gifts. One person may be good at drawing, another at writing. We are blessed also with spiritual gifts like truthfulness and kindness. Our gifts are all good because they come from God. A kitchen helper is as necessary as a doctor. But when gifts are used for the wrong reasons they become harmful. Think of a repairman who uses his skills to pick a lock and steal someone else's goods.

In the Bible (Matthew 25:14-30), Jesus tells about three workers who were given talents (money) to take care of while their master was away. The workers were given one, two or five talents and told to make money with them. When the master came back, he praised the worker whose five talents had become ten and the worker whose two talents had become four. The last worker was afraid of his master. He hid the talent he had received. The master scolded him, calling him a "wicked and lazy slave."

Though the story is about money instead of spiritual and bodily gifts, it tells us that we must use our gifts or we may lose them. They will dry up and blow away. Michelle and the prisoners who gave the play used their gifts to make people happy.

Today, find a spot where you can sit quietly and think about your gifts. Are you using them well? Are you losing any of them because you don't use them?

PRAYER

> *Dear God, at my birth you gave me gifts to make me a good*
> *person and to help others. In my childhood, my parents and*
> *teachers helped me use my gifts. Now that I am an adult, help*
> *me put my gifts to good use. Make my gifts grow like the two*
> *workers' talents. Bless prison staff like Michelle and all*
> *prisoners who use their gifts to help others.* AMEN.

ACTIVITY

- Try planning a program at the prison. The topic could be a holy season, like Ramadan or the Jewish Passover. Or you could ask someone from one of the prison clubs to give a talk; you could plan a panel on a news event. Ask friends to help you choose what to do. Then ask for help from the prison staff. Next plan the program. The prisoners will be sure to clap and praise you for the program you give!

- In the library, find stories about people you like. What gifts do they have and use? Write about them in your notebook. It will help you think about your own gifts.

Volunteer Appreciation Day

Once a year the Adrian prison holds Volunteer Appreciation Day. It's a time when prisoners and staff give a dinner to thank the volunteers who help at the prison.

The staff make certificates for the warden to sign, plan the menu for the dinner and walk with volunteers to the dining room. Prisoners help by making centerpieces for each table. Those who work in the greenhouse bring houseplants in hanging baskets as gifts for the volunteers.

The only prisoners at the dinner are heads of clubs and committees and those who teach classes. Prisoners who can't go to the dinner thank volunteers by video. Prison groups, like the Spanish and lifers' clubs, choose someone to say a short thank you on the video.

The program begins after dinner with the showing of the video. The warden speaks about the volunteers and how they help prisoners. The program ends with the warden giving out certificates. The volunteers then choose plants from the greenhouse.

SCRIPTURE READING

But wanting to justify himself, [the scholar of the law] asked Jesus, "And who is my neighbor?" Jesus replied, "A man was going down from Jerusalem to Jericho, and fell into the hands of robbers, who stripped him, beat him, and went away, leaving him half dead. Now by chance a priest was going down that road; but when he saw him, he passed by on the other side. So likewise a Levite, when he came to the place and saw him, passed by on the other side. But a Samaritan while traveling came near him; and when he saw him, he was moved with pity. He went to him and bandaged his wounds, having poured oil and wine on them. Then he put him on his own animal, brought him to an inn, and took care of him. The next day he took out two denarii, gave them to the innkeeper, and said, 'Take care of him; and when I come back, I will repay you whatever more you spend.' Which of these three, do you think, was a neighbor to the man who fell into the hands of the robbers?" He said, "The one who showed him mercy." Jesus said to him, "Go and do likewise." (Luke 10:29-37)

REFLECTION

Volunteers are good people who can't walk away from the needs of others. What begins as a simple act of goodwill often becomes a deeper, lifetime choice. In the Bible (Luke 10:30-37), Jesus tells of a man who was attacked by robbers. They beat him, took his money and left him lying by the road half dead. A priest and a Levite went by but didn't stop. They didn't want to get mixed up in that mess! Why, the man would need a doctor, food and money!

The Good Samaritan, one of a group of people called the Samaritans that the Jews didn't like, went by the same way. He saw the man and felt sorry for him. He washed the man's sores, set him on his own donkey and led him to an inn. The Samaritan told the innkeeper to care for the man's sores and his other needs. "And when I come back," the Samaritan said, "I will repay you."

The story of the Good Samaritan shows us that doing good isn't just a one-time thing. It takes time and commitment. We must help a person in trouble for as long as it takes.

Today, think of prison volunteers who've made your life easier because they kindly offered to help.

PRAYER

The Bible has many stories of people who helped others in God's name. Ask these good people to pray for you.

Good Samaritan, you helped a sick man when others walked away from him. Ask God to help me serve everyone in need no matter who they are.

Three Wise Men (Matthew 2:1-6), you followed a star through long, hot days to lay gifts at the feet of Jesus. Ask God to help me use my gifts to help those in need.

When Jesus was at Bethany in the house of Simon the leper (Matthew 26:6-13), you, unknown woman, washed his feet with oil. Ask God to help me serve others with loving care, because I see in them the face of Jesus. AMEN.

ACTIVITY

• The Adrian prison has a greenhouse for growing houseplants. Across the street from the prison is a big garden where vegetables are raised for the prison and for a food bank for the poor. Find out if your prison has a garden or greenhouse. Ask if you can help. Even if you can't go outside the walls, you can help by washing and packing vegetables.

• Ask to start a volunteer club. Find out what you can do to help make the prison a better place. Your activities director may find ways you can help people in town. You could fold and stuff envelopes, make favors for dinner trays at rest homes, make gifts to sell at fundraisers for the poor.

Bon Appétit

Bon Appétit is a good place to eat. The food is tasty and very cheap. The small prison café called Bon Appétit serves lunches made by prisoners in a cooking class. Anyone who works at the prison may bring a friend to lunch. All they have to do is call ahead and pay a small bill. No tips, please!

The café serves soup, salad, sandwiches, a drink and dessert. Prisoners in white wait on tables. They hope to work in a café when they are out of prison. Kitchen workers are learning how to cook. They want to become cooks in a café.

The class teaches prisoners how to work in a café and something even more important: Prisoners learn to be proud of their work. They feel good about giving food to hungry people. One of the prison cooks was so proud of what he had made that he told people at the café, "Try my lemon pound cake; I made it from scratch!"

SCRIPTURE READING

After this, Jesus went to the other side of the Sea of Galilee, also called the Sea of Tiberias. A large crowd kept following him, because they saw the signs that he was doing for the sick. Jesus went up the mountain and sat down there with his disciples. Now the Passover, the festival of the Jews, was near. When he looked up and saw a large crowd coming toward him, Jesus said to Philip, "Where are we to buy bread for these people to eat?" He said this to test him, for he himself knew what he was going to do. Philip answered him, "Six months' wages would not buy enough bread for each of them to get a little." One of his disciples, Andrew, Simon Peter's brother, said to him, "There is a boy here who has five barley loaves and two fish. But what are they among so many people?" Jesus said, "Make the people sit down." Now there was a great deal of grass in that place; so they sat down, about five thousand in all. Then Jesus took the loaves, and when he had given thanks, he distributed them to those who were seated; so also the fish, as much as they wanted. When they were satisfied, he told his disciples, "Gather the fragments left over, so that nothing may be lost." So they gathered them up, and from the fragments of the five barley loaves, left by those who had eaten, they filled twelve baskets. When the people saw the sign that he had done, they began to say, "This is indeed the prophet who is to come into the world." (John 6:1-14)

REFLECTION

Giving food with love makes us think of our parents and our childhood. Our parents gave us a place where we felt safe, a place where we didn't have to hide because we were afraid. They fed us warm food when we were sick. They fixed the food we liked for birthdays and other big days of the year. When parents don't feed children, both in body and soul, children grow up to spend the rest of their lives looking for the love they didn't get when they were young.

Jesus knew the human need to feed others. The Bible (John 6:1-15), tells the story of the loaves and fishes. Jesus had been talking to about five thousand people. It was getting late and the people were hungry. Jesus' friends didn't know what to do. They were afraid to send the people home without food. That could cause a riot! Nobody had any money. What to do? "There is a boy here who has five barley loaves and two fish," Andrew told Jesus, "but what are they among so many people?" Jesus knew he could feed everyone with the food the boy had brought. The people sat down and ate all they wanted. The leftovers filled twelve baskets!

Jesus did more than feed hungry people. He fed their souls by giving them a sign of his love. We are called to help others in the same way.

PRAYER

Dear God, you fed five thousand people on five barley loaves and two fish. I thank you for feeding me through my parents and the other caregivers in my life. Bless the people who cared for me so lovingly. Watch over prisoners and all people who feel that nobody wants them, nobody loves them. Help them to see that you love everyone you created. Bless my children and the children of the world. Help parents as they try to raise their children to be good people when they grow up. AMEN.

ACTIVITY

- The story of the loaves and fishes can be found six times in the Bible: Matthew 14:13-21; Matthew 15:32-39; Mark 6:30-44; Mark 8:1-10; Luke 9:10-17; John 6:1-15. Try to read at least one of these stories.

- One way of helping children is by reading to them. In the library, find children's stories, like "Jack and the Beanstalk," "The Ugly Duckling" and "Cinderella." What values are found in the stories? Are these the values you find in children's stories on television? In your notebook, write the answers to these questions. Write a letter to the newspaper telling what you learned.

- Children's stories are selling well today. Write a story for children. Make the story easy to read. Be sure it has a good ending. When you finish the story, send it to a magazine for children. Be proud of your work!

Reception

Every day dozens of visitors walk past the reception desk at the entrance to the state prison. They come to visit prisoners in the cells behind the steel doors of the security area (bubble). The prison entrance isn't a very nice place. The bright lights and hard floors make it seem very cold. Lockers fill one wall; along the other wall are soda and junk food machines. Near the security area are rows of hard chairs.

A typical visitor comes in the early evening after a long, tiring bus ride from her home to the prison. She is a wife with her children. If this isn't her first visit, she knows what paperwork is needed and what kinds of things she can bring her husband inside the prison.

For the newcomer, the desk can be a problem. If she hasn't filled out the right papers or doesn't know visiting hours, she won't get into the prison. She will go back home tired and angry because her trip was useless. Even if she gets into the prison, she may have to leave outside the gifts she brought for her husband. Bringing gifts may break prison rules.

After the woman leaves the desk, she goes to the security area. The wait may be a long one. There may be many visitors ahead of her. The children will cry and ask to go home. The chairs will become very hard!

When the wife's name is called, she and her children enter the bubble and are patted down. An officer checks their mouths and shoes. The goods they bring in will be X-rayed. The baby's diapers will be changed just in case drugs are hidden there.

The family next goes to the visitors' room where the husband and father waits for them. Happy is the wife whose husband asks about her health and the children's classes in school. All too often the talk is all about the husband, his needs, problems and legal appeals. When the wife leaves the prison, she may feel more tired than when she went in.

SCRIPTURE READING

> A capable wife who can find?
>   She is far more precious than jewels.
> The heart of her husband trusts in her,
>   and he will have no lack of gain.
> She does him good, and not harm,
>   all the days of her life.
> She seeks wool and flax,

and works with willing hands.
She is like the ships of the merchant,
    she brings her food from far away.
She rises while it is still night
    and provides food for her household
    and tasks for her servant girls.
She considers a field and buys it;
    with the fruit of her hands she plants a vineyard.
She girds herself with strength,
    and makes her arms strong.
She perceives that her merchandise is profitable.
    Her lamp does not go out at night.
She puts her hands to the distaff,
    and her hands hold the spindle.
She opens her hand to the poor,
    and reaches out her hands to the needy.
She is not afraid for her household when it snows,
    for all her household are clothed in crimson.
She makes herself coverings;
    her clothing is fine linen and purple.
Her husband is known in the city gates,
    taking his seat among the elders of the land.
She makes linen garments and sells them;
    she supplies the merchant with sashes.
Strength and dignity are her clothing,
    and she laughs at the time to come.
She opens her mouth with wisdom,
    and the teaching of kindness is on her tongue.
She looks well to the ways of her household,
    and does not eat the bread of idleness.
Her children rise up and call her happy;
    her husband too, and he praises her:
"Many women have done excellently,
    but you surpass them all."
Charm is deceitful, and beauty is vain,

but a woman who fears the LORD is to be praised.
Give her a share in the fruit of her hands,
   and let her works praise her in the city gates.
(Proverbs 31:10-31)

REFLECTION

The Bible in the above passage from Proverbs tells about "the perfect wife," or "the capable wife" or "the valiant woman." "Strength and dignity are her clothing," the Bible says. Her children are well fed and warm. The wife, never lazy, plans for the future by working late and selling her extra goods. Because of her, her husband is rich and well liked in the town.

The prisoner's wife and the woman in the Bible are alike in many ways. Both women care about their family. They are not lazy. They love deeply and from their love comes the strength to work long hours to hold the family together. The prisoner's wife, like the woman in the Bible, is a valiant woman whose husband and children should "rise up and call her happy."

Think about your family today. When they visit, are you the loving husband or father who wants to hear everything about the family since their last visit?

Do you make it hard for your family by making collect calls asking for clothing and other goods?

PRAYER

MOTHER, I bless you for loving me even when I didn't love myself.

WIFE and LOVER, I bless you for loving me, for caring for our children and for visiting me in prison.

CHILDREN, I bless you as a sign of God's blessing on our marriage. May you always feel happy and loved.

GOD, *bless my family. Help me to love and care for them.*
AMEN.

ACTIVITY

- Try making greeting cards today. You don't need to be an artist to make one. Use whatever you have. Write a poem for every card you make. Be sure to make an envelope for mailing the card. Mail the cards between family visits.

- In the library, look for stories, poems or jokes to tell your family the next time they visit. The stories, poems and jokes will make your family laugh. The visit will be good for everyone.

- Say thank you many times today. It will help you get ready for your next family visit.

- Ask your chaplain for ideas on how to keep your family strong while you are in prison.

Calendars

Prisoners love calendars, the big ones with bright pictures. The calendars mark the days, weeks and years they've been in prison. They tell them of the time left before a parole board hearing or the blessed time when they will be set free.

A prison volunteer found that churches often sent out free calendars each year. The volunteer liked to give the calendars to prisoners in his class. When one class came to an end, the volunteer saw that his students wanted more than one calendar. They would give the extra ones to friends, the volunteer hoped. It was easy for the volunteer to get more calendars from his friends. They were glad someone could use the calendars; the prisoners were glad to get them.

Before classes began the next month, prison volunteers got a letter from the assistant deputy warden (ADW) in charge of activities. No more calendars or other presents could be brought into the prison by volunteers, the letter said. No more holy cards or pens for prisoners. No more calendars!

The volunteer asked about the ruling. The ADW said, "It's a prison rule; we just weren't following it." A few months later, someone told the volunteer why the prisoners wanted extra calendars. They sold them to other prisoners and used the money for drugs or other things they shouldn't have!

SCRIPTURE READING

People were bringing little children to him in order that he might touch them; and the disciples spoke sternly to them. But when Jesus saw this, he was indignant and said to them, "Let the little children come to me; do not stop them; for it is to such as these that the kingdom of God belongs. Truly I tell you, whoever does not receive the kingdom of God as a little child will never enter it." And he took them up in his arms, laid his hands on them, and blessed them. (Mark 10:13-16)

REFLECTION

God is simple, a being of endless wisdom whose word is truth. In God there is no lying or cheating. Jesus asks us to be simple of heart like the God who made us: "Truly I tell you, whoever does not receive the kingdom of God as a little child will never enter it" (Mark 10:15). Jesus isn't telling us to be childish; he asks us to be simple and honest like a child. Children are simple beings who don't know how to fool others. They have to be taught to cheat.

As adults, we can't always say what's on our minds, but when we speak our words should be honest. We shouldn't try to fool others.

Simple trust in God will keep us from being afraid to tell the truth. Jesus tells us, "Do not worry about your life, what you will eat or drink, or about your body, what you will wear.... Look at the birds of the air; they neither sow nor reap nor gather into barns, and yet your heavenly Father feeds them" (Matthew 6:25-26).

PRAYER

When you want to hide your real reasons for asking for something, ask God to help you speak simply, using the words of or words spoken to the strong men and women of the Bible.

John the Baptist: "The one who is more powerful than I is coming after me; I am not worthy to stoop down and untie the thong of his sandals" (Mark 1:7).

God, help me to practice the honesty of John.

Mary: "Here am I, the servant of the Lord; let it be with me according to your word" (Luke 1:38).

God, help me to obey you the way Mary did.

Joseph: "Son of David, do not be afraid to take Mary as your wife, for the child conceived in her is from the Holy Spirit" (Matthew 1:20).

God, help me, like Joseph, to live in peace with the daily events that I'm not able to change.

Jesus: "Why were you searching for me? Did you not know that I must be in my Father's house?" (Luke 2:49).

Jesus, help me to tell others the Good News of God's love by always being honest and telling the truth. AMEN.

ACTIVITY

- As you meet and talk to people today, think of yourself as Jesus walking with his friends. What would Jesus want you to say to them?

- What birds, plants or flowers do you like best? Choose three of each kind. In the library, find all you can about the ones you chose. Make a booklet about what you've learned. If you are studying plants, for example, you could write a short story about each one, telling the kind of soil and the amount of water it needs. Make a drawing of the plant, showing all its parts. If it is a flowering plant, show petals, pistil and stamen. Find poems about plants to add to your booklet or write one of your own. On the last page of your booklet, write a prayer or copy a Bible reading. Give your booklet a name. If you like the booklet you have made, make copies and use them as gifts.

Doug

Prisoners are always happy to have visitors. One visitor, Michigan State Representative Doug Spade, talked to a class at the Adrian prison. He brought with him Mike, his helper, and Toby, his seeing-eye dog.

The prisoners liked Doug. He was open and honest with them, never trying to cover up problems in the legislature or laws that needed to be changed. If he couldn't answer a question, he wasn't afraid to say so. "Doug doesn't talk like a politician," one prisoner said. Prisoners, like many other people, don't trust politicians.

The high point of the evening came at the end of class when Doug let the prisoners pat Toby. A dozen hands reached out to touch the animal lying quietly at Doug's feet.

SCRIPTURE READING

And God said, "Let the earth bring forth living creatures of every kind: cattle and creeping things and wild animals of the earth of every kind." And it was so. God made the wild animals of the earth of every kind, and the cattle of every kind, and everything that creeps upon the ground of every kind. And God saw that it was good.

Then God said, "Let us make humankind in our image, according to our likeness; and let them have dominion over the fish of the sea, and over the birds of the air, and over the cattle, and over all the wild animals of the earth, and over every creeping thing that creeps upon the earth."

So God created humankind in his image,
in the image of God he created them;
male and female he created them.

God blessed them, and God said to them, "Be fruitful and multiply, and fill the earth and subdue it; and have dominion over the fish of the sea and over the birds of the air and over every living thing that moves upon the earth." (Genesis 1:24-28)

REFLECTION

Pets can soothe and calm sick children and old folks. When they visit hospitals and rest homes, pets can make a sick person's blood pressure drop. Children are more peaceful after petting an animal. Pets like Toby can do even more: They can help the blind walk safely across city streets.

Animals are part of God's beautiful world. The Book of Genesis in the Bible tells how the world was made in God's seven days. In the first days, God made the earth and sky, land and water. God filled the water with fish and the air with birds. On the sixth day God made the animals of the earth. Only then did God make people. God rested on the seventh day, and the day was holy.

God didn't stop after those seven days. He stays with all the things he made, loving them into the beautiful beings they were meant to be.

Take a quiet walk around the yard today. While you're walking, think of all the things God made and how they all work smoothly together. We are part of God's world; we must do our part to keep it beautiful.

PRAYER

When you come back from your walk, pray these words from Psalm 104:31-35 in the Bible:

> *May the glory of the LORD endure forever;*
> *may the LORD rejoice in his works—*
> *who looks on the earth and it trembles,*
> *who touches the mountains and they smoke.*
> *I will sing to the LORD as long as I live;*
> *I will sing praise to my God while I have being.*
> *May my meditation be pleasing to him,*
> *for I rejoice in the LORD. . .*
> *Bless the LORD, O my soul.* AMEN.

ACTIVITY

• In the library, find out all you can about seeing-eye dogs: what types make the best ones, how they are trained and who trains them. If you know someone who is going blind, tell that person what you have learned.

- Ask the chaplain if you can talk about our world at the next prayer service. If the chaplain lets you do so, begin planning your talk. You could begin with the prayer you have just said. Think of ways prisoners can help keep our world lovely, like picking up paper in the yard or walking on the sidewalk instead of on the grass. Write out your talk, making sure to keep it short; it will make your point clearer. Give the chaplain a copy of your talk. Make any changes the chaplain thinks you should make.

- When you give the talk, be sure to speak slowly and clearly. Show by your words and actions how much you love our world and want to keep it beautiful!

PART FIVE

Life on the Outside

Yahweh has leaned down from the heights of his sanctuary,

has looked down from heaven to earth,

to listen to the sighing of the captive,

and set free those condemned to death.

—Psalm 102:19-20, THE NEW JERUSALEM BIBLE

Dan

Dan was paroled from prison a few years ago. Now he's busy at his work: laying carpets and linoleum. He doesn't write to his old friends in prison. "I'm too busy," he says. The real reason he doesn't write could be because of a friendship that failed.

Dan tried to be a friend to the other prisoners. He listened to what they had to say. He read the stories they wrote. Dan worked on the prison newspaper. He began by laying out the pages, then moved up to reporter and finally became the editor's helper. When the editor was sent to another prison, Dan asked for his job. Another prisoner, a friend of Dan's, also wanted the job.

Then one day Dan was called to the prison office and shown a piece of paper found on the floor of one of the classrooms. It trashed the officers and the newspaper staff. The paper had Dan's name on it.

Dan was shocked. He had never seen the paper before! He didn't write it, he told the guards. Yet they sent him to the prison jail for a few days. While Dan was in jail, the officers followed up on a tip and found that the letter was written by the prisoner who wanted to be editor. Neither of the two men got the job; it went to someone else.

SCRIPTURE READING

But Naomi said, "Turn back, my daughters, why will you go with me? Do I still have sons in my womb that they may become your husbands? Turn back, my daughters, go your way, for I am too old to have a husband. Even if I thought there was hope for me, even if I should have a husband tonight and bear sons, would you then wait until they were grown? No, my daughters, it has been far more

bitter for me than for you, because the hand of the LORD
has turned against me." Then they wept aloud again.
Orpah kissed her mother-in-law, but Ruth clung to her.

So she said, "See, your sister-in-law has gone back to
her people and to her gods; return after your sister-in-
law." But Ruth said,

> "Do not press me to leave you
>   or to turn back from following you!
> Where you go, I will go;
>   Where you lodge, I will lodge;
> your people shall be my people,
>   and your God my God.
> Where you die, I will die—
>   there will I be buried.
> May the LORD do thus and so to me,
>   and more as well,
> if even death parts me from you!"

When Naomi saw that she was determined to go with her,
she said no more to her. (Ruth 1:11-18)

REFLECTION

Prison is a poor place to make friends. Prisoners move around
a lot. They aren't in one place long enough to have friends.
Because they don't know each other, they can't be trusting.
Where there is no trust, there can be no friendship.

The Bible tells the story of three friends, Naomi and her
daughters-in-law Orpah and Ruth. They knew each other for
many years before they became friends. Then the three women
became widows. Naomi told her daughters-in-law to go back to
their families where they would find new homes and new husbands. Orpah went back to her home, but Ruth would not. She
stayed with Naomi, saying:

Where you go, I will go;
Where you lodge, I will lodge;
your people shall be my people,
and your God my God.
Where you die, I will die—
there will I be buried. (Ruth 1:16-17)

Take time today to think about the Bible story. What values did these women have that you would like to find in friends? Think about Dan. Why was he afraid of making friends? Think about the friends you made before you went to prison. What can you do to keep their friendship?

PRAYER

Our Father in heaven, I ask you to bless my friends as you did Naomi, Orpah and Ruth. Help me to find new friends. When friendships don't work, keep me from being hurt and afraid to make new friends. AMEN.

ACTIVITY

• Write to a friend today. Tell the person how happy you are to have a friend. Fill the letter with funny stories and jokes. Try not to talk about your problems or ask for money.

• Look up the word, "friendship." Does it fit your idea of friendship? Write down what you look for in a friend. Are you a friend to yourself? Try to be the kind of friend you want your friends to be.

Cellblock 1

The prison in Adrian has one cellblock for prisoners who will soon be paroled. These prisoners sometimes work in the town. They clean gutters, mow lawns or rake leaves. An officer always goes with them. The prisoners wear orange T-shirts with the word prisoner on the back. They can have no money or anything else in their pockets.

One hot day last summer the town was in an uproar. The newspaper said that a prisoner, we'll call him Orange, had gone to a store nearby when the officer wasn't looking. He got a can of beer, went back to his workplace, sat down and drank the beer. The guard didn't know that Orange paid for the beer by picking up cans. What Orange didn't know was that someone had called the police.

Orange's actions could have led to more prison time. But officials didn't press charges. The uproar in the city died down, and Orange is now out on parole. He can drink beer whenever he chooses.

SCRIPTURE READING

At that time Jesus went through the grainfields on the sabbath; his disciples were hungry, and they began to pluck heads of grain and to eat. When the Pharisees saw it, they said to him, "Look, your disciples are doing what is not lawful to do on the sabbath." He said to them, "Have you not read what David did when he and his companions were hungry? He entered the house of God and ate the bread of the Presence, which it was not lawful for him or his companions to eat, but only for the priests. Or have you not read in the law that on the sabbath the priests in the temple break the sabbath and yet are guiltless? I tell you, something greater than the temple is

here. But if you had known what this means, 'I desire
mercy and not sacrifice,' you would not have condemned
the guiltless. For the Son of Man is lord of the sabbath."
(Matthew 12:1-8)

REFLECTION

It's easy to like Orange. Everyone likes a cold drink after working in the sun. Orange broke no laws. He bought his beer; he
didn't try to run away. He makes us think of times when we've
broken rules that seemed silly to us. Think of the driver who
wants to get home in a hurry. He comes to a red light that seems
to last forever. No one is around. Who wouldn't want to go
through the light?

Jesus knew our human wants. The above story from
Matthew in the Bible tells about a Saturday when Jesus and his
friends were hungry. They began eating the grain in the fields.
Now Saturday was a holy day for the Jews, just like our Sunday.
Jews didn't work on that day. They told Jesus that he was breaking the law. Jesus laughed at silly laws like this one. Yet he kept
just laws. He paid temple taxes (Matthew 17:24-27) just like
everyone else.

Unlike Jesus, Orange didn't look ahead to see whether his
actions could hurt others. The newspaper story about him could
make people think all prisoners were bad people. Yet prisoners
helped the town by raising vegetables for the poor and giving
flowering plants to shut-ins.

Orange's actions could have led to pain or even death. A
worker or a shopper might have had a gun and used it, thinking
Orange had run away from prison!

Today, think about a time when you acted without thinking.
If you had to do it over again, would you act in the same way?

PRAYER

Learn this prayer. Say it when you need God's help to act wisely.

> *My Lord Jesus, I know that you love me with an everlasting love. I know that my foolish actions can hurt others and myself. When I want to break prison rules or even try to run away, help me to see the foolishness of my actions. Be with me, Jesus, as I try to live wisely today.* AMEN.

ACTIVITY

- Take part in a game with other prisoners today. It could be basketball or softball in the yard or a game of cards in the activities area. Before you make each move, think of how it will affect others. Will this move lead to good clean fun, or will it cause a fight?

- In your notebook write about the game you just played. Were your actions wise or foolish? Think about what you have learned when you need to make bigger choices.

Bubble

The doors leading into the prison security area (bubble) can be very scary. There are two sliding steel doors, one leading to the outside and the other into the prison. An officer behind a plate glass window opens the doors; another officer searches visitors as they enter the security area. Some officers search more carefully than others. One officer even stops visitors who have Kleenex in their pockets. "That's against the rules," she says. Another officer may not even check the pockets of a visitor.

A few years ago, one of the women officers felt a lump near a visitor's breasts. The woman was eighty years old. The lump turned out to be a small bag of cocaine. The woman, of course, didn't get into the prison! Because of her age, she got off easy. She paid only a small fine.

We'll never know why the woman acted as she did. The prisoner she was visiting may have asked for drugs. "If you don't bring me any, I'll get even with you," he could have said. Or the woman could have been to blame. She might have wanted to sell drugs to the prisoners and make a little money. Whatever the reason, the woman's actions were wrong and very foolish.

SCRIPTURE READING

"Then the kingdom of heaven will be like this. Ten bridesmaids took their lamps and went to meet the bridegroom. Five of them were foolish, and five were wise. When the foolish took their lamps, they took no oil with them; but the wise took flasks of oil with their lamps. As the bridegroom was delayed, all of them became drowsy and slept. But at midnight there was a shout, 'Look! Here is the bridegroom! Come out to meet him!' Then all those bridesmaids got up and trimmed their lamps. The foolish said to the wise, 'Give us some of your oil, for our lamps are going out.' But the wise replied, 'No! There will not be enough for you and for us; you had better go to the dealers and buy some for yourselves.' And while they went to buy it, the bridegroom came, and those who were ready went with him into the wedding banquet; and the door was shut. Later the other bridesmaids came also, saying, 'Lord, lord, open to us.' But he replied, 'Truly I tell you, I do not know you.' Keep awake, therefore, for you know neither the day nor the hour." (Matthew 25:1-13)

REFLECTION

In the Bible in Matthew 25, Jesus tells the above story of ten bridesmaids. Five were foolish, and five were wise. The five foolish bridesmaids didn't bring extra oil for their lamps, so they had to buy more. By the time they got back from the market, everyone had gone; they couldn't go to the wedding.

The bridesmaids acted foolishly, but we can see how it happened. We all act foolishly at times. That's part of being human. Think of the friend who left by car to spend a weekend with his aunt but forgot to bring his suitcase! Or the child who planted an Easter egg thinking it would sprout more eggs!

The most foolish of all actions, however, is using or selling drugs. Drugs hurt our bodies; they change our minds and hearts so that we no longer act like human beings. We will do anything, even hurt or kill people, to get a "fix."

Today, think about the foolish bridesmaids and the even more foolish woman trying to bring drugs into the prison. Think of your own foolish actions. Did you ever use drugs? Are you using them now? What can you do to help yourself?

PRAYER

Lord, Jesus, I know that taking drugs is a foolish act. The few hours of happiness it gives lead only to pain for myself and those around me. Help me to find happiness in better ways—in the beauty of nature, a good book, the love of my family and friends. Bless and help drug users who are trying to break the habit. Bless their families and all who suffer from drug abuse. Help me to walk straight ahead on the path that leads to you, my God. AMEN.

ACTIVITY

- Write to your family today. Fill the letter with stories about the little things that make you happy. Ask your family to pray that you will stay far away from drugs.

- In the library, find out all you can about drugs and how they hurt people.

- If you have a friend who uses drugs, tell him how bad they are, but don't hurt his feelings. If he gets angry, talk about something else. Be careful! Drug users could hurt you if they don't like what you're saying.

Mark

Mark is a good-looking man with a fresh open face. He likes to talk, but he also listens carefully to what others have to say. He makes people feel that they have good ideas. Good friend or con man? He could be either.

Sadly, Mark has used his many gifts to con others, even volunteers. He got a volunteer to give him her home phone number. Then he spent hundreds of dollars making calls paid for by the volunteer. He conned another volunteer into giving him money for a paralegal class.

Things only got worse when Mark got out on parole. He didn't want to return home where people knew him. They were too smart to be conned. He asked a friend to rent an apartment for him, help find him a job and enroll him in college music classes, all at the friend's expense. Things were fine for a few months. Then the college found drums and guitars missing; stores wanted the money for goods Mark had bought on credit. When he was asked for money, Mark ran from his apartment and hid at a girlfriend's place.

When the police arrested Mark, they charged him with robbery and breaking parole. They also talked to the red-faced friend who had let himself be fooled by a con artist.

SCRIPTURE READING

It happened, late one afternoon, when David rose from his couch and was walking about on the roof of the king's house, that he saw from the roof a woman bathing; the woman was very beautiful. David sent someone to inquire about the woman. It was reported, "This is Bathsheba daughter of Eliam, the wife of Uriah the Hittite [Joab's armor-bearer]." So David sent messengers to get her, and she came to him, and he lay with her. (Now she was purifying herself after her period.) Then she returned to her house. The woman conceived; and she sent and told David, "I am pregnant."...

In the morning David wrote a letter to Joab, and sent it by the hand of Uriah. In the letter he wrote, "Set Uriah in the forefront of the hardest fighting, and then draw back from him, so that he may be struck down and die." As Joab was besieging the city, he assigned Uriah to the place where he knew there were valiant warriors. The men of the city came out and fought with Joab; and some of the servants of David among the people fell. Uriah the Hittite was killed as well. (2 Samuel 11:2-5, 14-17)

REFLECTION

Many times each day we try to get people to do things for us. That doesn't mean that we're con artists; it's just a way of working with others to make life easier. If we're lonely and would like a friend to fix dinner, we might call and tell her she's a great cook! Or we might be more open and say: "If you fix dinner tonight, I'll take you out to dinner next week." Working with others in this way can be good for everyone.

But it's wrong when we use other people as things—like the rolling of the dice—to get what we want. We roll the dice, hoping we'll get lucky and win big. The dice are only things for our use; they don't feel pain or shame. But people aren't dice. They have feelings. They can be hurt. As people of faith, we are called to love each other, not to use another person for our own selfish needs.

In the Bible (2 Samuel), there is a story as bad as any crime story on television. King David, who had everything he could ever need, still wanted more: the lovely Bathsheba, wife of Uriah the Hittite, a soldier in the king's army. When the king called Uriah to him and asked about the army, Uriah wasn't fooled. He knew the king wanted his wife. He stayed with the king's guard instead of going home. David wanted to kill Uriah when he was alone. When he couldn't do that, David wrote to Joab, the head of the army. David told Joab to put Uriah in the middle of the fighting where he would be killed. After Uriah was killed, David married Bathsheba. But God, the Bible says, was not pleased with David.

Think about the stories of Mark, David and Bathsheba. Have you ever used other people for your own selfish needs? Was anyone hurt by what you did?

PRAYER

My God, you made everyone in your own likeness. Help me to see everyone I meet as a mirror reflecting your goodness. Walk with me today, God, as I try to live as the good person you want me to be. AMEN.

ACTIVITY

- In your notebook rewrite the story of David and Bathsheba. Show what David could have done to please God. What about Mark? How should he have acted toward the people who were trying to help him?

- The next time you turn on the television, check out the first five ads you see. Do the ads try to make people do something they shouldn't do? If you don't like what you see, write to the TV station and tell them what you don't like. Do you have any ideas about how to make ads better?

- Instead of watching television one night this week, ask a few friends to talk about the stories in this reflection. Ask one friend to read the story of Mark; ask another to read the part about David and Bathsheba. Talk about the readings, ending with the prayer found in the reflection, or make up one of your own.

AFTERWORD

[**E**lijah] got up, and ate and drank; then he went in the strength of that food forty days and forty nights to Horeb the mount of God. At that place he came to a cave, and spent the night there.

Then the word of the LORD came to him, saying, "What are you doing here, Elijah?" He answered, "I have been very zealous for the LORD, the God of hosts; for the Israelites have forsaken your covenant, thrown down your altars, and killed your prophets with the sword. I alone am left, and they are seeking my life, to take it away."

He said, "Go out and stand on the mountain before the LORD, for the LORD is about to pass by." Now there was a great wind, so strong that it was splitting mountains and breaking rocks in pieces before the LORD, but the LORD was not in the wind; and after the wind an earthquake, but the LORD was not in the earthquake; and after the earthquake a fire, but the LORD was not in the fire; and after the fire a sound of sheer silence. When

Elijah heard it, he wrapped his face in his mantle and
went out and stood at the entrance of the cave. Then there
came a voice to him that said, "What are you doing here,
Elijah?" (1 Kings 19:8-13)

In this part of the Bible, we meet Elijah, who is running away
from his enemies. He had won a showdown with the followers
of the god Baal, and he knew he would be killed if he were
captured. He ran to Mount Horeb and hid in a cave. Though
Elijah could escape from his enemies, he could not escape from
God. God called Elijah, saying, "What are you doing here,
Elijah?"

As he did to Elijah, God calls everyone, including the
people you've met in this book, to leave their prison-like caves,
many of them self-made. God asks you to go stand on the
mountain and wait for him.

But God will not be found in the wind of windy words that
hurt other prisoners; nor will God be found in the violence and
hate of a prison riot or the sharp fire of a gunshot that brings
death to an escaping prisoner.

God will be found only in the gentle breeze stirring in the
silence of the human heart. Once you have found God, God
will ask, "What are you doing here?" In what way are you
called—even in the limited space of a prison—to do God's
work? How can your life today—at this very moment—reflect
the glory of a God who loves you even though you have failed

him so many times?

At some point in life, everyone is called to answer that question. The response may lead to a deeper love of God, a better understanding of self and a respect for God's holy creation.

Take courage. Have no fear. God will never leave you. God's peace be with you.